CLOSING PAGE

DISCLAIMER

The information provided in this book is for general informational purposes only. It is meant as a complement to enhance the reader's understanding.

SHE MEANS BUSINESS

UNLEASHING WOMEN'S FINANCIAL POWER

BY

CECILIA HANSON

SHE MEAN BUSINESS: UNLEASHING WOMEN'S
FINANCIAL POWER

TABLE OF CONTENTS

SHE MEAN BUSINESS: UNLEASHING WOMEN'S FINANCIAL POWER

INTRODUCTION

A tectonic change is taking place in the boardrooms of business and the corridors of power. A dramatic transition is taking place in the business and financial sectors, which were formerly governed by a single narrative. The basic underpinnings of trade and economic influence are being altered by an emergent force that is powerful and unstoppable. Women are that force—determined, strong, and destined for greatness.

"She Means Business: Unleashing Women's Financial Power" takes the reader on a fascinating tour through this revolutionary time. It serves as a rallying cry for the many women who have been unfairly underrepresented, underpaid, and underestimated in the world of business and finance for far too long. It examines the incredible accomplishments and limitless potential of women who have dared to break down barriers, change the status quo, and set their paths to financial success.

The message in the headline is strong: women are not only joining the corporate world; they are reshaping it. This book is a call to action to observe, accept, and take advantage of the paradigm change that is "women in business." It's a proclamation that women are serious businesspeople.

In the pages that follow, we'll take a journey into a world where women are leading economic transformation, where their triumphant tales will inspire you and their financial empowerment tactics will hold your attention. A testimony to the incredible skills of women, their unbreakable spirit, and their unquestionable financial power, "She Means Business" is more than simply a book.

This book is a comprehensive guide that gives women the tools, knowledge, and inspiration they need to succeed in the world of business and money, covering everything from mastering the art of negotiation to creating personal brands that resonate to navigating the complexities of money management to encouraging mentorship and networking.

But "She Means Business" is a movement, not simply a book. It's an exhortation to action for women to realize their financial potential, escape the confines of gender prejudice, and take control of the world economy. It's confirmation that women are serious about business in every way. Prepare to be inspired, informed, and transformed as we set off on this inspiring adventure through the world of women in business and finance.

A monument to the increasing wave of female empowerment that will transform businesses, economies, and communities for future generations, "She Means Business" is more than just a book. The moment has arrived to release women's economic potential, and this book will serve as

your compass on the incredible
journey that lies ahead.

CHAPTER 1

BREAKING THROUGH BARRIER

Women have battled The Glass
Ceiling, an imperceptible yet
persistent force, since the dawn of
humanity. Numerous women have
been prevented from reaching their
full potential in the professional
sector by this figurative barrier. But
there are many amazing cases of

women who broke this glass ceiling throughout history.

Women like Oprah Winfrey, who defied all odds to go from being a radio personality to being a media tycoon, or Mary Barra, who became the first female CEO of a major automaker, The phrase "glass ceiling" refers to invisible hurdles that keep women from advancing to senior management positions in the corporate sector.

Women still struggle greatly to overcome these intangible hurdles, despite the advancements they have achieved in education and job growth throughout time. The commercial sector has always been controlled by men, and women have been restricted to lower-paying less respected jobs.

Women didn't start to make substantial strides in the economic sector until the middle of the 20th century, due to the women's rights movement. However, only roughly 5% of Fortune 500 company CEO roles are held by women today. The difficulties that women encounter in the professional sector are numerous and intricate.

Unconscious bias is one of the biggest problems when people have established views or prejudices that affect their perceptions and behavior. This may result in women being passed over for promotions, not being paid equally to their male colleagues, or not being invited to important meetings where decisions are made.

The dearth of networking and mentoring options for women is a serious issue as well. Many women find it difficult to locate mentors and sponsors who can help them as they make their way through the professional world. In addition, women frequently aren't included in informal networks that have a big influence on access to opportunities and job progression.

Despite the obstacles, several women have broken through the "glass ceiling," achieved incredible financial success, and paved the way for subsequent generations of women. These women are trailblazers who have broken down barriers and pushed the envelope to accomplish their objectives.

Real-Life Success Stories of People Defying the Odds

Think about Susie. Kim Riley's amazing journey as the creator of the mobile monetization platform Aquto She has been recognized as one of the Top 100 Female Founders by Entrepreneur Magazine, and Verizon, AT&T, and Netflix are among the clients of her business. Riley's accomplishment is proof of the tenacity and diligence needed to be successful as a woman in business.

Cynthia Marshall, the first black woman CEO in the NBA, is another success story. In 2018, she was named CEO of the Dallas Mavericks basketball franchise. By encouraging inclusiveness and diversity in the workplace, she has revolutionized the corporate culture while serving as a leader.

These tales serve as examples of the tenacity needed to overcome the challenges faced by women in the economic sector. They serve as a reminder of the progress accomplished by women and as motivation for the next generation to persist and shatter the glass ceiling.

Determining the Value of Representation Breaking down the hurdles that women encounter in the economic sphere depends critically on representation. Women need to witness other successful women in leadership roles to be inspired and motivated to pursue achievement that is comparable to their own.

Furthermore, decision-making is enriched by the different viewpoints and experiences that women in leadership positions bring to the table. As diversity makes use of the many viewpoints, experiences, and insights of various people, problem-solving and decision-making become more successful.

Additionally, representation can aid in dismantling gender stereotypes and implicit prejudices that women encounter. When women succeed in leadership jobs, it disproves the stereotype that they are unable to perform well in important positions.

Additionally, it encourages inclusion and diversity in the workplace, creating a welcoming and encouraging atmosphere for people from all backgrounds. To overcome the obstacles that women encounter in the economic sector, representation is essential.

It challenges prejudices and biases, encourages other women to set greater goals, and adds other viewpoints to decision-making. It will take a team effort to promote and support women in leadership positions to achieve genuine gender equality in the economic sector.

Lessons Learned and Next Steps

After learning about the origins of the glass barrier and the experiences of women who have overcome it, it's time to take action. Make an inspiration board with images of successful women who motivate you. Use it as a reminder in visual form of what is possible.

- Networking: Make connections with successful female colleagues in your industry. To create a support network, go to networking events or join online communities.
- Education: Commit to continuous learning and skill development to improve your credentials and self-assurance.

Create a plan for accomplishing your professional or company goals after defining them. Keep in mind that, despite its existence, the glass ceiling is breakable. You can overcome it and accomplish more on your financial path if you have grit, support, and a good strategy. We'll provide you with the methods and tools you need to accomplish it in the upcoming chapters. So let's get started and release your financial potential!

CHAPTER 2

THE RISE OF WOMEN IN BUSINESS

In the corporate sector, women's participation and influence have been rising gradually over time. It is impossible to overlook the considerable economic contributions that women make as well as their increasing impact across a range of industries. This chapter will examine the prominent patterns and data that demonstrate the growing representation of women in leadership positions as well as the important lessons that can be drawn from them.

Economic Impact: Women as a Catalyst of Growth

Through innovation and entrepreneurship, women today significantly contribute to economic progress. Women own or jointly own 40% of all businesses in the United States, creating 8 million jobs and $1.8 trillion in yearly income, according to the National Association of Women Business Owners (NAWBO).

Additionally, studies suggest that organizations with more women in leadership roles typically do better financially and have healthier organizational cultures. Having more women in business is good for the economy as a whole as well as for the women who work there.

Trends and Statistics: The Ascension of Women in Leadership

Despite the advancements, it is important to recognize that women continue to confront substantial obstacles in their quest for equality in the workplace. However, the following informative and motivating data and trends demonstrate the increase in women in several industries:

- With 37 women in the top executive positions at their organizations in 2020, the proportion of female Fortune 500 CEOs set a record high.

- Women now occupy 23.7% of board seats for the S&P 500, reflecting a steady rise in the proportion of women on corporate boards.

- Degrees in business and management are being pursued by more women. Women make up 50.3% of students in undergraduate business schools and 46.5% of students in MBA programs in the United States.

- With female CEOs in charge of businesses like IBM, General Motors, and Hewlett-Packard Enterprise, women are driving the IT sector.

These patterns and figures demonstrate how women are increasingly overcoming the obstacles that have previously limited their chances of success in the corporate sector. Instead, they are demonstrating that they are qualified and competent leaders who can promote development and innovation across a range of industries.

Real-Life Examples

The advancement of women in positions of leadership goes beyond statistics and trends. Women who have broken the glass ceiling and attained positions of power and influence have many amazing tales to share.

Ginni Rometty, the first woman to serve as CEO of IBM, serves as one illustration. IBM strengthened its investments in cybersecurity, cloud computing, and artificial intelligence under her direction, driving the company's emphasis on innovation and technology.

Rosalind Brewer, the current CEO of Walgreens Boots Alliance and the previous CEO of Sam's Club, is another illustration. She is the first black woman to hold the position of CEO at a Fortune 500 corporation and has been named one of Forbes' most influential businesswomen.

These women's success stories demonstrate that perseverance, tenacity, and a clear goal are necessary for attaining success in the economic world.

Actionable Advice and Takeaways

It is critical to keep pushing for fair representation and opportunity for all women as more women take on leadership roles. The following suggestions for concrete actions that people and organizations may take to help women in business:

- Learn about the structural obstacles that prohibit women from rising in the economic sector and work assiduously to remove them.

- By offering direction, counsel, and chances for advancement, mentor and sponsor women in your company.

- By actively seeking out and respecting different ideas and experiences, you may foster a culture of diversity and inclusion.

- Speak up in favor of laws that encourage gender equality at work, such as equal pay, maternity leave, and flexible scheduling.

- If you want to be in a leadership position, aggressively seek out leadership development opportunities.

- Promote inclusiveness and gender diversity in your company or sector. Positive change may be influenced by your voice.

- If you want to pursue business, do extensive study and planning. Take inspiration from the success tales of other female business owners

Conclusion

Women and the economy as a whole gain from the big and exciting trend of more women in business. Women's contributions to innovation, entrepreneurship, and leadership are crucial for fostering diversity and inclusion in the workplace as well as for accelerating growth. We must keep encouraging and empowering women as they strive for professional success.

Not only are women succeeding in business, but they are also prospering and changing sectors. You are better prepared to negotiate your path to financial success if you are aware of the economic contributions that women make and keep up with trends and statistics. The tactics and tools that will enable you to control this rising tide and release your financial power will be covered in greater detail in the chapters to follow.

CHAPTER 3

THE FEMALE ENTREPRENEURIAL SPIRIT

Women now have significant opportunities to manage their financial destinies and achieve the work-life balance they desire through entrepreneurship. In many nations, women-owned firms are expanding more quickly than those owned by men, and female entrepreneurs are breaking down barriers and smashing glass ceilings to succeed in a wide range of industries. We will discuss why entrepreneurship is particularly empowering for women in this chapter and identify notable female business leaders who have made important contributions to their industries.

Entrepreneurship as Empowerment

Entrepreneurship is about taking charge of one's life, not only founding enterprises, and it may be a particularly powerful route for women. Giving women the freedom to determine their financial futures without being constrained by social norms, offers a road to financial independence.

Additionally, it gives women the chance to shatter the glass barrier and create their possibilities without needing approval. The ability to manage family and profession on one's terms is one of the key benefits of entrepreneurship for many women. Women who own their enterprises frequently concentrate on finding solutions to social problems to make a positive difference in their communities and the wider world.

Women who explore entrepreneurship have the freedom to take charge of their financial destinies, design flexible work schedules, and follow their hobbies. Women-owned firms are more likely than men-owned enterprises to place a higher priority on work-life balance and a sense of purpose. They frequently start with a vision to improve their communities and the globe.

In addition, entrepreneurship enables women to overcome structural obstacles that have historically hindered them from succeeding in their jobs. Through entrepreneurship, students are given the freedom to build the enterprises and jobs they desire on their terms.

Profiles of Women Entrepreneurs

There are several motivating accounts of female company owners who overcame challenges to succeed in the corporate world. Let's get to know some amazing women business owners who have not only embraced it but have also succeeded in the face of difficulties:

- Nasty Gal, a fashion firm that began as an eBay store and expanded to become a multi-million dollar business, was founded by Sophia Amoruso. She currently oversees Girlboss, a website that offers information and motivation for female entrepreneurs.

- The creator of the cult-favorite cosmetics product Glossier, Emily Weiss, started the company as a blog. Weiss has developed a devoted following and expanded her company thanks to her distinctive approach to beauty and relentless concentration on her clients.

- A digital health platform for women called Maven Clinic was founded and is led by Kate Ryder. After becoming frustrated with the healthcare system throughout her pregnancy, Ryder founded the business because she saw an opportunity to improve the experience for other women.

- Sara Blakely is Spanish. She created Spanx, which revolutionized the underwear market. She started off selling fax machines but persevered and used creativity to become the youngest self-made female millionaire.

- The Body Shop's Anita Roddick The Body Shop was established by Anita Roddick and combines skincare goods with moral principles. Her dedication to social responsibility and sustainability left a lasting legacy.

- HuffPost's Arianna Huffington The Huffington Post, which Arianna Huffington co-founded, revolutionized internet journalism. She is an advocate for health and has pushed for women to give self-care a priority.

- OWN Network, Oprah Winfrey Oprah Winfrey is a media and business pioneer. She is a role model for tenacity and perseverance and is credited with creating an empire from scratch, including her television network.

These women's experiences demonstrate the variety of routes that female company owners can follow to succeed in the corporate world. Their tenacity, commitment, and inventiveness serve as examples of the effectiveness of entrepreneurship as a vehicle for empowerment and transformation.

Actionable Advice and Takeaways

There are various concrete measures that women who want to pursue business may take to get started:

- Find a passion you wish to pursue or a need in your community.
- Conduct in-depth market research to identify your target market and rivals.
- Look for mentors and resources, such as networking opportunities, company incubators, and accelerators.

- Make a business strategy and approach potential clients to seek their input on your concepts.
- Create a solid team and foster connections with partners and clients. Go looking for finance options, such as loans, grants, and investors.
- Recognize that entrepreneurship entails risk. Continue ahead and take lessons from your failures.

Conclusion

Women may now manage their financial destinies, design flexible work schedules, and follow their hobbies with the help of entrepreneurship. The experiences of successful female business owners serve as examples of the variety of career options available to women. Women may overcome obstacles, smash glass ceilings, and succeed in business by having access to tools and assistance. We may anticipate a society in which women have even more possibilities and financial power as more women start successful enterprises.

You already have an entrepreneurial spirit that is just waiting to be released. Your path starts with a single step, regardless of whether you envision running a small business or starting a startup. The next chapters will go into further detail about the practical aspects of entrepreneurship and give you the resources you need to realize your goals. Prepare to start a life-changing path toward financial empowerment.

CHAPTER 4

MASTERING MONEY MANAGEMENT

For women who want to take charge of their financial destinies, learning how to handle money is an essential skill. Knowing the ins and outs of saving, investing, and budgeting is crucial, whether you're just starting in your career or want to retire comfortably. We'll give you a thorough crash course in financial literacy in this chapter, along with investing tactics designed specifically with women's specific financial needs and objectives in mind.

Financial Literacy: Your Foundation for Success

It's crucial to understand your present financial condition before you begin investing or saving for the future. This entails setting up a budget, keeping tabs on your expenditures, and figuring out where you can reduce your costs. You'll develop a deeper understanding of your financial patterns and be better equipped to manage your money by making a budget and keeping track of your expenditures.

Having a firm grasp of fundamental financial ideas like compound interest, diversification, and risk management is crucial in addition to budgeting. You may examine various investment possibilities and make educated judgments about your investments with the aid of this information.

Investment Strategies for Women: Navigating the Financial Landscape

While many of the fundamentals of investing apply to both men and women, women frequently confront particular difficulties and possibilities. Women, for instance, must plan for a longer retirement since they typically live longer than men. Women frequently earn less than men throughout their careers, which may affect their capacity to put money aside and make investments.

Focusing on building a diverse portfolio is one investment approach for women. You may lower overall risk and improve your chances of long-term growth by diversifying your assets across several asset types. This might entail making investments in stocks, bonds, property, or other assets.

Utilizing financial options designed exclusively for women is another tactic. For instance, several businesses provide investing solutions designed to assist women in accumulating money and achieving their financial objectives. You may locate assets that support your principles and financial goals by looking for these opportunities.

Whatever investing techniques you decide to adopt, it's critical to never lose sight of your long-term financial objectives. Women may attain financial stability, freedom, and success with a thorough grasp of financial literacy and a well-thought-out investment strategy.

Takeaways and Action Steps

It's time to act now that you've learned crucial financial literacy information and examined investing options specifically geared toward women.

- Make a Budget: Put in place a budgeting strategy that matches your lifestyle and financial objectives.
- Open a savings account and start investing, even with small sums, to get started saving and investing.
- Consistency is crucial. Continue your education by taking online classes, attending seminars, and reading books about personal finance and investing.

- Create a strategy to reach your financial goals after defining them clearly.
- Review often and make necessary adjustments.
- Seek professional advice. For individualized advice, think about speaking with a financial advisor with experience in women's financial planning.

CONCLUSION

In conclusion, women of all ages and socioeconomic levels must learn effective money management skills. You may attain financial stability and independence for the rest of your life by taking the time to learn about budgeting, investing, and saving, as well as by creating a sound investment plan suited to your requirements and objectives. Therefore, get started right away on developing a sound investment plan and financial literacy. You'll be grateful to your future self.

Never forget that being an expert in money management is a journey, not a goal. Your financial success will be built on the abilities you acquire in this chapter. In the chapters that follow, we'll look at more tips and tricks for navigating the financial world with assurance and purpose.

CHAPTER 5

NEGOTIATING LIKE A PRO

In this chapter of "She Means Business: Unleashing Women's Financial Power," we'll discuss how mastering the art of negotiation can help women progress in their jobs and succeed in their business endeavors. Negotiation is both an art and a talent. We'll go into useful methods and advice while discussing the particular difficulties that women frequently encounter in negotiations and providing solutions for them.

Every woman should learn how to negotiate to thrive in both her professional and entrepreneurial endeavors. Salary discussions, contract renegotiations, and the buying and selling of products and services are all examples of bargaining. However, being a skilled negotiator is not simple, especially for women. When negotiating, gender prejudice frequently exists, making it challenging for women to obtain the favorable terms they deserve.

So how can women combat gender bias difficulties and bargain effectively? Here are some helpful tactics and advice for haggling like a pro:

- Knowing your worth is the first step to bargaining well. Find out how much your qualifications and expertise are worth, then use that information as a negotiating tool. Don't underestimate your worth because of your gender or any other circumstance.

- Active listening is an effective negotiating tactic. Pay attention to both what is said and what is not expressed as well. You can find common ground and hidden interests by actively listening.

- Establish specific goals: Clearly state the goals of your negotiations. What do you want to accomplish, and what is your ultimate goal? Your bargaining tactics will be guided by a clear objective.

- Establish trust: Trust is the foundation of any negotiation. Building trust with the other party may contribute to the creation of a more pleasant environment, increase cooperation, and produce better results. Find areas of agreement, pose inquiries, and listen intently.

- Being well prepared is essential to bargaining well. Study the market circumstances, your counterpart's demands and interests, as well as their negotiating tactics. Additionally, be certain of your objectives, best-case scenario, and other options.

- Communicate firmly: Women frequently make the mistake of being overly courteous or hesitant. Women must convey their requirements assertively during negotiations, making it clear what they want and why they deserve it. Additionally, they must develop good conflict management skills and maintain confidence throughout the negotiation.

Think innovatively and from both sides' perspectives when negotiating. Finding a solution that works for both sides is more important than winning at the cost of the other party. Women must exercise creative thinking, be open to other options, be willing to make concessions when they are called for and work to discover win-win solutions.

Don't be scared to be quiet during negotiations. Prompting your opponent to divulge more or make compromises can be a potent strategy.

How Women Can Speak Up for Their Rights in the Face of Gender Bias

Women need to learn how to overcome gender prejudice, which has the potential to greatly affect the result of a negotiation, in addition to being proficient in practical negotiating skills and strategies. Here are some pointers to assist women in speaking out for themselves:

- **Be mindful of Gender Bias:** Women may encounter it unintentionally through interruptions, being passed over, or having their worries minimized. Knowing these warning flags and how to spot them in a negotiation is crucial.

- **Building Confidence:** Acknowledge your value and get confident in your bargaining skills. The secret to a good negotiation is confidence.

- Don't apologize for your needs. Women frequently experience guilt or awkwardness while speaking out for their needs. To attain the outcomes you want, it is essential to advocate for what you feel you are entitled to.

- Not aggressiveness, but assertiveness, is a key quality in negotiations. Be careful not to be confrontational, but don't be afraid to stand up and fight for what you believe in.

- **Negotiate Collaboration:** Adopt a collaborative approach to bargaining, which is frequently thought of as more socially acceptable for women. A more positive and effective environment may be produced through collaborative negotiation.

- **Seek Mentoring:** To receive insightful advice and support, think about seeking mentoring from seasoned negotiators, both men and women.

- **Use assertive language:** Women who assert themselves in negotiations and refrain from apologizing or downplaying their demands frequently get better results.

- **Create networks:** Women can create networks with other women who have experienced comparable difficulties in getting over gender prejudice. Knowing that other women have experienced the same discrimination might help one feel supported and united.

Lessons Learned and Next Steps

It's time to put your negotiating talents to use now that you have knowledge of the art of negotiation and methods for overcoming gender bias.

- Practice negotiating. Whether it's pay discussions or commercial transactions, look for opportunities to practice negotiating in your personal and professional life.

- Keep a notebook of your negotiations. Keep a notebook of your negotiations and note what went well and poorly. Utilize this criticism to improve your strategy.

- Role-playing activities can help you gain confidence and skills in negotiations. Try them out with a dependable friend or mentor.

- Join negotiation workshops: To expand your knowledge, look for

training   programs   and
workshops in negotiation.

- Connect with other women who
  have   successfully   negotiated
  their way to job development via
  mentoring and networking. Take
  advice from them and look for a
  mentor.

CONCLUSION

Women   must   master   the   art   of
negotiation if they want to develop in
their   professions   and   businesses.
Women who recognize their worth,
develop   relationships,   plan
meticulously, speak assertively, and
think imaginatively are better able to
bargain. It takes knowledge, boldness,
good   language,   and   network

development to overcome gender prejudice. It might be difficult to learn how to bargain like a pro, but with perseverance and practice, women can overcome these difficulties and succeed.

Your professional and financial lives can be drastically improved by learning how to negotiate. As you develop your negotiating skills, you'll find that you can overcome obstacles gracefully and get results that are in line with your objectives. We'll keep arming you with crucial information and tools to excel in the business and financial worlds in the upcoming chapters.

CHAPTER 6

BUILDING YOUR BRAND

A clever slogan or elaborate logo is only a small part of your brand. It combines your reputation, values, subject-matter knowledge, and personality. The distinct personality and reputation you establish in the eyes of others is your brand.

Creating a powerful personal brand is crucial if you want to thrive in your job or business. What makes personal branding so crucial? Here are a few advantages to consider:

- **Stand Out from the Crowd:** In a crowded or competitive field, having a strong personal brand can help you be noticed by potential clients, employees, or consumers. You may stand out from the crowd and find your niche by exhibiting your abilities, values, and viewpoints.

- **Build credibility and trust:** Your target audience will be more receptive to you if you have a strong personal brand. People are more inclined to trust you and see you as an authority in your industry when they perceive that you have a strong reputation, a track record of success, and insightful observations.

- **Increase Your network and chances:** A strong personal brand can help you access more resources and career chances.

Your brand may make it simpler to establish worthwhile connections and broaden your network, whether it's through speaking engagements at conferences, job opportunities, or working with other professionals.

How do you go about creating your brand now that you are aware of its advantages? Here are some pointers:

- Establish your brand. Determine your special talents, principles, and character attributes first. Consider your unique selling proposition and the benefit you may provide to others.

- Establish a unified message. From your website to your social media sites, your brand should be consistent. Make sure your messaging is concise and consistent with the character and values of your brand. Make use of social media.

- Building and strengthening your brand may be done effectively with the help of social media. Select the platforms that would best serve your target market and concentrate on producing interesting, informative material that highlights your knowledge and personality.

- Get your audience involved. Developing a personal brand involves more than simply self-promotion. It's about creating deep ties with other people. Engage with your audience, answer their questions and comments, and provide value wherever you can.

- Keep changing. Who you are and what you stand for should be reflected in your brand. Your hobbies, abilities, and values may vary throughout time, and it's good to develop and adapt. A personal brand requires consistency, time, and work to develop.

However, with the strength of personal branding on your side, you may improve your company and career chances and leave a lasting impression in your sector.

Real-life examples of personal branding

1 Gary Vaynerchuk-The CEO of VaynerMedia and a digital marketing specialist, Gary Vaynerchuk He has created a personal brand around his commercial success, inspirational writing, and mastery of social media.

He is noted for having a positive attitude and an engaging demeanor.

2. Oprah Winfrey-Oprah's sincerity, wit, and empathy are the cornerstones of her brand. She has established herself as an iconic figure in entertainment, charity, and personal growth by creating a media empire centered on her voice and principles.

3. Neil Patel is a well-known marketer who has created a personal brand with his knowledge of digital marketing and SEO. On his blog and social media, he frequently offers insightful information, and he has developed a devoted following of

companies and marketers who turn to him for guidance.

Actionable advice

- Spend some time reflecting on your distinct personality traits, values, and strengths. Create a list of them and utilize it as the basis for your brand.

- Create a consistent message. Ensure that your message is consistent throughout all channels, such as your website, social media, and promotional materials.

- Make judicious channel selections. Create useful material

that appeals to your target audience's preferences, and keep an eye on the platforms they utilize.

- Get your audience involved. Engage with your audience, answer their questions and comments, and provide value wherever you can.

- Keep changing. Who you are and what you stand for should be reflected in your brand. Never be scared to try new things and adapt as you gain new knowledge and develop new talents.

Takeaways and Action Steps

Following your understanding of the value of personal branding and the significance of having an online presence, consider taking the following steps:

- **Self-Reflection**: Give yourself some time to reflect. What principles, interests, and skills do you want your brand to convey?

- **Establish your audience:** Clearly state who your target market is. With your brand, who are you seeking to connect with?

- Develop a content strategy for your online presence by creating a content plan. How often will you distribute your material, and what kind of content will you produce?

- **Professional Development:** Keep advancing your knowledge and abilities in the area you have chosen. Your brand gets stronger the more knowledgeable you are.

- **Request Feedback:** Consult with friends or mentors to get their opinions on your brand and online presence. Utilize their suggestions to further hone your brand.

CONCLUSION

Success in your job or business depends heavily on the development of your brand. You may build a strong personal brand that improves your prospects and has a significant influence in your industry by identifying your distinctive talents, crafting a consistent message, using social media, interacting with your audience, and growing over time.

Your brand is a resource that may help you succeed in your professional and entrepreneurial endeavors. You'll be better able to create a lasting impression on individuals you meet by developing a powerful, honest, and consistent personal brand and utilizing the digital channels at your disposal. We'll continue to look at methods for achieving financial success in the upcoming chapters.

CHAPTER 7

MENTORSHIP AND NEW WORKING

Women nowadays need more than just education and diligence to succeed in the fast-paced corporate environment. They require direction, assistance, and inspiration from mentors who have already experienced it. Mentors are seasoned experts who offer direction and counsel to assist women in growing their abilities, overcoming obstacles, and achieving their objectives. They may share their experiences, offer insightful criticism, and support women as they successfully negotiate the challenges of the professional world.

It is impossible to overestimate the importance of mentors for women's job advancement. According to research, women who have mentors are more likely to succeed in their jobs and report feeling more satisfied with their work. Additionally, they are more likely to hold leadership roles and receive greater pay. Women may discuss their work goals with a mentor in a secure environment where they can also share their struggles and get advice on how to get past them. Mentored women can increase their self-esteem, sharpen their talents, and widen their networks in the workplace.

Additionally important to women's job advancement is networking. Strong professional connections can open doors to new possibilities, perceptions, and suggestions. Making meaningful relationships with people who can support you in achieving your career objectives is the purpose of networking, which is more than merely meeting new people. It takes time, effort, and a planned strategy to effectively network.

Attending trade shows and conferences is one way to network. These gatherings offer chances to network with other industry experts, discover market trends and best practices, and raise your profile among important stakeholders. Having a solid online presence is crucial for developing your brand. This includes setting up a business LinkedIn profile, participating in online discussions, and starting a personal blog or website.

Joining leadership groups or professional organizations is another successful networking tactic. These clubs provide chances to interact with other like-minded individuals, take part in industry debates, and develop your skills through seminars and training sessions. You can also get in touch with previous coworkers, teachers, or professionals in the field to get suggestions, criticism, or guidance.

Takeaways and Action Steps

Here are some concrete measures to support your mentorship and networking efforts now that you are aware of the value of mentors and have some networking tips:

- Find potential mentors: Look for mentors who have expertise in your sector or subject. Look for people you respect and appreciate.

- Establish a mentoring connection. Be humble while speaking with possible mentors, and be sure to make clear your expectations for the connection.

- Develop a networking strategy. Create a networking strategy outlining the occasions and activities you'll attend to broaden your professional network.

- Attend workshops and seminars to learn new skills. Enroll in workshops and seminars that offer networking possibilities.

- Active listening is a skill that should be honed when networking. Demonstrate a sincere interest in the experiences of the individuals you encounter.

CONCLUSION

For women to advance in their careers and build successful businesses, networking and mentoring are crucial. Having a mentor may help you navigate obstacles and inspire you to accomplish your goals. A systematic strategy is necessary for effective networking, which includes going to events, establishing an internet presence, and joining trade associations. Women may increase their professional network, develop new abilities, and advance in their jobs by utilizing these tactics.

Networking and mentoring are two more effective strategies that may help you advance both personally and financially. You may locate a community that will assist you in achieving your goals by actively searching out opportunities to interact with people and cultivating these relationships. We'll continue to look at methods for achieving financial success in the upcoming chapters.

CHAPTER 8

BALANCING BUSINESS AND PERSONAL LIFE

The majority of individuals find it difficult to strike a balance between their personal and work lives. Managing your workload while also taking care of your loved ones and yourself at the same time is difficult. To live a healthy, fulfilling, and successful life, this balance must be preserved. We will cover key strategies in this chapter for finding the ideal balance between your professional and personal lives

Life-Work Balance

Finding a balance between your personal and professional lives is the first topic we'll cover. The majority of us are prone to prioritizing our jobs over everything else in the fast-paced, competitive world of today. However, using this method frequently might result in fatigue and stress, which can then have an impact on our personal lives. Setting limits and making time for yourself, your family, and friends are essential for maintaining a healthy work-life balance.

The inability to say "no" is one of the main reasons for work-life imbalance. It's critical to realize that saying no occasionally is acceptable, especially when doing so starts to negatively impact your physical and emotional well-being. By establishing sensible priorities and goals, you may also maintain equilibrium. You can manage your time successfully by having a clear vision of what you want to do and setting priorities appropriately. To arrange time for work, family, and self-care, another strategy is to build good time management skills. Calendars and to-do lists are useful tools for staying organized.

Draw distinct lines separating your personal and professional lives. To make sure they are respected, let your coworkers and clients know about these boundaries. Forget about feeling guilty about taking time for yourself. Recognize the importance of self-care for your overall performance. At work and home, assign chores when you can. When assistance is required, don't be afraid to ask. Determine your highest priority in both your personal and professional lives. The things that are most important to you should receive your attention.

The Path to Resilience Through Self-Care and Wellness

Taking care of oneself is crucial to striking a balance between work and life. To live a healthy and full life, one must practice self-care. If you are not physically or mentally fit, it will be difficult for you to function successfully in your professional life. It is not selfish to take care of oneself; resilience and success need it. Here are some self-care strategies and advice to put your emotional and physical health first:

- Regular exercise not only keeps you healthy but also lowers stress and elevates your mood.
- Get adequate sleep since it can affect your general health, creativity, and productivity. Be

certain to obtain 7-8 hours of sleep every night.

- Eat well: A balanced, nutritious diet is essential for preserving one's mental and physical well-being.
- Practice mindfulness: You may lower your stress and increase your mental clarity by using mindfulness practices like yoga, deep breathing, meditation, and deep breathing.
- Make time for your interests by engaging in pastimes and activities that make you happy and relaxed. A potent stress reducer is following your passions.

Takeaways and Action Steps

Here are some actions you can take to create and maintain a balanced life now that you are aware of how important work-life balance and self-care are:

- Consider your present work-life balance as you evaluate it. Do any parts that still require work?

- Set Boundaries: Clearly outline the lines between your personal and professional lives. Tell other people about these limitations.

- Make self-care a priority by adding regular self-care activities to your schedule and treating them like essential appointments.

- If you're having trouble maintaining balance or feeling well, don't be afraid to ask for help from mentors, friends, or experts.

- Regular Evaluation: Assess your work-life balance regularly and make any improvements. Over time, your requirements and situation could alter.

Conclusion

A healthy and meaningful life depends on being able to successfully balance your career, business, and personal life. Set limits, choose priorities, and take care of yourself. You may strike the appropriate balance and live a successful, contented life by paying attention to the advice given above.

Making self-care and well-being a priority while juggling work and personal obligations is crucial since it's a lifelong process. Your ability to manage the responsibilities of your job or business and attain long-term financial empowerment will improve if you take care of your physical and mental health. We'll continue to look at methods for achieving success and happiness in your financial path in the upcoming chapters.

CHAPTER 9

OVERCOMING ADVERSITY

Every worthwhile endeavor comes with its share of obstacles and failures. We ladies have frequently encountered a variety of challenges that may have slowed down our progress toward our objectives.

But it's crucial to understand that no matter what the situation, no matter how difficult it may appear, we have the power and resilience to go through it. The trait that distinguishes outstanding women from others is the capacity to recover and endure in the face of hardship.

We will examine the experiences of women in this chapter who overcame their challenges with tenacity and resilience. We will also talk about useful tips and techniques that may foster our resilience and give us the willpower to overcome challenges.

Resilience and Persistence: Overcoming Obstacles

Resilience is the capacity to overcome difficulties, and it's a trait that many successful women possess. Let's be motivated by their tales:

Four-time Olympic winner Lindsay Vonn has endured a great deal of hardship throughout her skiing career.

She underwent surgery for a severe knee injury she sustained in 2013, which nearly put an end to her career. She battled valiantly to stand up again yet she would not give up. She won her 20th World Cup championship in 2016, which is an accomplishment that can only be characterized as amazing.

Oprah Winfrey has also experienced hardships throughout her life, such as deprivation, abuse, and prejudice. She worked arduously to create an empire, becoming one of the most successful media moguls in the world, yet she refused to give in to her circumstances.

Malala Yousafza, who was shot by the Taliban for supporting girls' education, showed remarkable fortitude by continuing her work. She later became the youngest recipient of the Nobel Prize in history.

J.K. Rowling experienced financial difficulty as a single mother before becoming famous as the creator of the Harry Potter books. She also received rejection letters from multiple publishers.

Vera Wang began her career as a skilled figure skater before switching to the fashion business later in life. She overcame financial obstacles and naysayers to create a prosperous fashion company.

Michelle Obama became the first African American First Lady of the United States despite experiencing racial and gender discrimination as a child. She currently works to promote women's rights and education.

The perseverance of these ladies is just one illustration of its power. They had to overcome obstacles that may have prevented them from making progress, but they didn't give in. They put forth a lot of effort, overcame many obstacles, and came out stronger and more prosperous than before.

Resources for Resilience: Overcoming Obstacles

Not everyone is born with the ability to be resilient. However, we can cultivate this trait and improve our resilience in the face of challenges with the appropriate tools and mentality. Adversity cannot be avoided, yet it is possible to develop resilience. Here are some helpful tips for overcoming obstacles in life:

- Accept the Situation: Occasionally, events occur that are beyond our control. We must acknowledge the reality of the situation and concentrate all of our efforts on finding answers.

- Create a Support System: Having a network of people to lean on can help us get through difficult times. Be in the company of individuals who will inspire and motivate you to continue. Create a solid support system of close friends, relatives, mentors, and peers who can offer moral support and direction in trying times.

- Maintain a Positive Attitude: The key to recovering is positivity. Work to identify answers while concentrating on the areas you can control.

- Practice Self-Care: Developing resilience requires taking care of oneself. Make sure you're getting enough sleep, eating well, and doing things that make you happy.

- Adaptability: Be open to change and flexible. When faced with difficulty, be open to novel strategies and fixes.

- Develop your problem-solving abilities. Break down problems into small steps, then take each one on individually.

- View failure as a stepping stone toward success by learning from your mistakes. Use mistakes and failures as chances to improve by learning from them.

Lessons Learned and Next Steps

Here are some concrete measures to help you develop and increase your resilience now that you've read about examples of resilience and learned strategies for overcoming hardship:

- Self-Reflection: Consider your own hardship experiences and how you handled them. What talents and abilities have you acquired?

- Resilience-Building Exercises: Incorporate resilience-building exercises into your daily routine, such as writing, meditation, or, if necessary, professional counseling.

- Seek inspiration from positive role models who have triumphed against hardship. Examine their experiences and make a note of their coping mechanisms.

- Mentoring and Support: Take into account asking for advice from a mentor or coach who may offer direction and support through trying moments.

- Recognize and appreciate your accomplishments, no matter how minor they may appear. Your perseverance is demonstrated by each step you take ahead.

CONCLUSION

The traits that distinguish successful women include overcoming hardship, growing resilient, and nurturing persistence. It's not about avoiding difficulties; it's about overcoming them and emerging stronger thereafter. We may build and improve our resilience with the correct methods and outlook, overcoming challenges to come out stronger and more prosperous than before.

Although it could put your fortitude to the test, adversity can also stimulate empowerment and progress. You will not only conquer problems with tenacity and perseverance, but you will also come out stronger and more competent than before. We'll continue to look at ways to succeed personally and financially in the chapters that follow.

CHAPTER 10

PAYING IT FORWARD

Do you recall the first time someone took you under their wing and assisted you on your path as a woman? Perhaps a teacher pushed you to follow your aspirations because they thought you had something special. Perhaps a manager took the time to walk you through the process and impart useful knowledge. Or perhaps a buddy was the one who helped you when you needed it most emotionally.

Regardless of the circumstances, there is a good probability that someone has had a significant impact on your life and helped you develop and accomplish your objectives. You may also realize how crucial it is for women to help and mentor other women as you reflect on your own experience.

Women Mentoring and Supporting Other Women: How Important Is It?

Amazing things may occur when women support one another. Women's distinctive viewpoints and experiences are crucial in forming the world in which we live. Women bring a plethora of information, talents, and perspectives to the table in a variety of fields, including politics, business, and daily life.

You may aid in supplying direction and assistance as they travel their journeys by mentoring other ladies.

Whether you are a seasoned professional or are just beginning your career, you may help others who might be going through a similar situation by providing them with insightful counsel and inspiration.

You may help remove obstacles in their way and provide them with chances to be successful in industries that have traditionally been controlled by men by mentoring other women. Give the younger generation your knowledge and experiences so they can learn to avoid frequent traps and progress more quickly. You may increase other women's self-worth and confidence through mentoring, empowering them to work harder to achieve their goals.

Both the mentor and mentee gain from the enlarged professional networks that result from mentoring connections. You may be assured that your impact will last long after your career is over by leaving a legacy of mentoring and assistance.

But mentoring is more than simply delivering advice; it's also about giving people chances. In our professional lives, women may encounter particular obstacles and difficulties, such as lower pay, fewer job advancements, and fewer leadership positions. By encouraging other women, we may contribute to the removal of these restrictions and expand the options available to women.

Activism and Advocacy: Changing the World

Through advocacy and activity, we may help bring about positive change in our communities and professions, in addition to helping and mentoring other women. This can take many different forms, such as speaking up about significant topics or participating in neighborhood organizations.

Engaging in politics is an effective approach to changing things. Women's voices are frequently underrepresented in politics; therefore, by supporting or running for office, we can make sure that our opinions and experiences are taken into account. We may also fight for laws that help women, such as equal pay and policies that support working parents.

Other avenues for change are not related to politics. You can volunteer for groups that promote women's rights or strive to prevent gender-based violence. As a professional or influencer, you may utilize your position to spread knowledge about significant topics. By promoting fair treatment and opportunity, you may also help other women in your field.

Activism and advocacy are effective strategies to support constructive change in your community and profession. Promote equal compensation for equal effort, gender equality in the workplace, and chances for women in leadership positions. Create or take part in initiatives that pair up seasoned women with those who are just starting their careers.

Encourage educational programs that encourage young women and girls to pursue careers in STEM (science, technology, engineering, and mathematics). Promote inclusion and diversity in your field, calling for equitable representation and equal opportunity for everyone. Think about charitable initiatives that assist organizations and causes that promote equality and empowerment for women.

Lessons Learned and Next Steps

Here are some actions you can take to pay it forward and have a good influence as you get ready to finish this book:

- **Find mentoring opportunities:** Look for chances to guide other women in your field or neighborhood. Give them your advice and encouragement so they can accomplish their objectives.

- **Participate in advocacy efforts:** Participate in advocacy and action campaigns that share your values and convictions. Drive good change by using your voice and influence.

- **Create mentoring programs:** If you have the knowledge and resources, you might want to think about starting mentorship programs in your company or community.

- Contribute to organizations and projects that empower women and advance gender equality to support women's causes.

- **Be an Ally:** Actively endeavor to foster an inclusive and encouraging workplace by supporting women from all backgrounds.

CONCLUSION

Women can empower and encourage one another, fostering a society where all women may prosper. We can make a difference and bring about good change in our communities and industries through mentorship, advocacy, or action.

Paying it forward is a means to help others as well as a way to achieve personal fulfillment and advance women's emancipation. Your deeds can serve as an example to others and start a beneficial chain reaction. Keep in mind that you are still on the path to financial empowerment and that you have limitless potential to influence others. Finally, keep working toward achievement and female empowerment, not just for yourself but also for the many women who will come after you.

As a result, the next time you notice a woman who might use some direction or assistance, don't be hesitant to reach out and lend a hand. We can build a better future for ourselves and the subsequent generation of women by working together.

CHAPTER 11

THE FUTURE OF WOMEN BUSINESS

In this last chapter of "She Means Business: Unleashing Women's Financial Power," we look into the future to examine how the business world for women is always changing. The potential for even more influence and transformation is present in this environment.

The importance of women in business has never been greater as we look to the future. Although we've made enormous strides in the direction of workplace gender equality over the years, there is still a long way to go. The good news is that women in business have a bright future and a real chance to have an even bigger effect in the years to come.

Entrepreneurship is one field where women are having a significant influence. Women are launching their businesses at a higher rate than men, and this trend is continuing. The number of women-owned firms in the US has climbed by 58% since 2007, according to research by American Express. This demonstrates that women are not only capable of operating profitable enterprises but also possess creative thinking and a strong desire to achieve.

Leadership roles are another area where women are having an influence. Women have shown themselves to be very capable leaders, offering a distinctive viewpoint and method of decision-making. It has been demonstrated that businesses with women in leadership roles do better financially, underscoring the need for diversity in leadership.

Despite these encouraging developments, women in business continue to face several obstacles. There is still a significant gender wage difference, and many women still experience bias and discrimination at work. This is why it's so important that we keep advocating for gender equality and helping women who are trying to make it in business.

What can we do, then, to ensure that women's futures in business are even brighter? Supporting women-owned businesses and making an attempt to do business with them are important first steps. Additionally, we may try to create workplaces that embrace diversity and seek to be free of prejudice and discrimination.

Finally, we can support more women who want to work in business by giving them the skills and tools they require. This includes access to money and funding, networking opportunities, and mentorship programs.

The fate of women in business ultimately rests with us. We can build a society where women have equal opportunity to achieve and make a difference if we work hard, with passion, and with a commitment to gender equality. Let's embrace our financial clout and keep working to bring about constructive change in the corporate sector.

Looking Ahead: The Changing Business Environment for Women

For women in business, the future is promising and is characterized by several fascinating themes. As more women enter the field of entrepreneurship, the number of female-led startups and firms is rising. In business boardrooms, women are also shattering glass ceilings and taking on leadership positions, confronting gender inequities at the top.

Women are driving innovation across a range of sectors by offering new viewpoints and approaches to difficult problems. Women are growing in strength as advocates for workplace equality, leading to significant discussions and regulatory adjustments. Women are working together and supporting one another, creating networks and alliances that increase their effect.

Action Item: Recognize your financial power.

We issue a call to action—a call to embrace your financial power and make a significant impact—because after reading this chapter, you may be asking how you might make a difference in the business world: Here are some concrete actions you can take:

- Have unflinching faith in your skills and potential for success by believing in yourself. Your financial power is greatly influenced by your sense of self-worth.

- Never stop developing and learning; do the opposite. To stay competitive in your profession, invest in your education and skill development.

- Mentoring and Support: Encourage other women while offering assistance to those in need. Someone's journey may change as a result of your advice.

- Change Advocate: Use your position to promote gender equality, diversity, and inclusion in your workplace and sector.

- Set an example for the next generation of women in business by doing so. Through your accomplishments and deeds, you may demonstrate what is possible.

- Support women-owned and women-led businesses by choosing to do business with them whenever you can.

- Promote gender equality by speaking out against prejudice and discrimination in the workplace and by backing laws that support it.

- Connect with other women in business by going to events and joining groups that promote networking.

- Invest in your education and growth by making the time to do so, whether through formal schooling or by looking for independent learning alternatives.

Lessons Learned and Next Steps

Here are some concrete measures you can take as you continue your path after finishing this book to embrace your financial power and influence the direction that women in business will go:

- **Set bold goals:** Clearly and aspirationally state your financial and professional objectives.

- **Create a support system:** Surround yourself with role models, friends, and allies who can offer advice and inspiration.

- **Stay Informed:** Keep abreast of market developments and trends, and keep studying throughout your professional life.

- Encourage diversity and gender equality in your workplace and sector by speaking out against prejudice and unfairness.

- Lead with integrity. Lead with honesty and integrity, motivating others with your dedication to progress.

CONCLUSION

You play a key role in the promising future of women in business. You not only contribute to your success but also the collective empowerment of all women as you embrace your financial power and make a difference. The trip ahead is yours to design; this book has served as a guide. Therefore, go out on your journey with self-assurance, tenacity, and the certainty that you have what it takes to succeed and motivate others to follow in your footsteps.

Recall that we are responsible for the future of women in business. Together, let's create a future where everyone has the chance to prosper.

CLOSING PAGE

We want to thank you for joining us on this life-changing journey as we close out "She Means Business: Unleashing Women's Financial Power" with this final chapter. You've studied the experiences of inspiring women who overcame adversity, the value of personal branding, the skill of negotiating, the value of mentorship, and the significance of work-life balance throughout this book. You now have a newfound knowledge of entrepreneurship, investment tactics, and financial literacy.

The journey, however, is far from over. Your journey to financial independence and personal success has just begun. You have a priceless toolkit in your hands, one that will guide you through the challenging world of business and finance by providing knowledge, inspiration, and useful guidance.

Keep in mind that using your financial power to improve your life and the lives of others is more important than simply accumulating wealth. It's about creating a legacy of achievement and equality, advocating for change, and empowering the subsequent generation of women.

We urge you to embrace your financial power going forward with courage, confidence, and tenacity. You are an essential component of the successful future that lies ahead for women in business. You'll not only accomplish your objectives by continuing to learn, develop, and lead with a purpose, but you'll also motivate others to achieve greater heights.

Women can truly reach their full potential and become powerful change agents in business with the right encouragement, tools, and education. All women should use this book as a call to action to take charge of their financial futures and realize their full potential. We can all benefit from a future that is more just and prosperous if we work together.

We are confident in your abilities and eager to witness the enormous contribution you will make to society at large and in the business world in particular. So, move forward confident that you can achieve greatness and unleash your full financial potential. Your journey has just begun, and there are countless possibilities.

We appreciate your participation in "She Means Business: Unleashing Women's Financial Power." In both your professional and personal endeavors, we wish you success, fulfillment, and happiness.

Sincere regards,

SHE MEAN BUSINESS: UNLEASHING WOMEN'S
FINANCIAL POWER

CECILIA HANSON